RELIQUARY

RELIQUARY

Abigail Wender

Four Way Books
Tribeca

for Rohan, Anna, Oliver

Library of Congress Cataloging-in-Publication Data

Names: Wender, Abigail, author.
Title: Reliquary : poems / by Abigail Wender.
Description: [New York] : Four Way Books, [2021] |
Identifiers: LCCN 2020037843 | ISBN 9781945588679 (paperback)
Subjects: LCGFT: Poetry.
Classification: LCC PS3623.E533 R45 2021 | DDC 811/.6--dc23
LC record available at https://lccn.loc.gov/2020037843

This book is manufactured in the United States of America and printed on
acid-free paper.

Four Way Books is a not-for-profit literary press. We are grateful for the assistance
we receive from individual donors, public arts agencies, and private foundations.

This publication is made possible with public funds from the
New York State Council on the Arts, a state agency.

We are a proud member of the Community of Literary Magazines and Presses.

Contents

I.

II.

III.

"A Robin Red breast in a Cage
Puts all Heaven in a Rage"

William Blake, "Auguries of Innocence"

I.

A Room

I was speeding along a familiar highway
to the village of no time,

no time to visit the ocean, ancient companion,
my lungs filled with its aching air,

no time for salty promises, mildewed sweaters and blankets,
cards that would not shuffle.

The closer I came to windmills and steeples,
the bluer the sky looked,

trees in brassy autumn.
I packed the patio furniture and penny drawer riffraff

I desired—
Indian head nickels, *pfennigs*, subway tokens,

a tiny cast-iron devil playing his tuba.
Descartes began by imagining the room emptied,

first chair, desk, candle, and at last his pen. When nothing remained, he considered his abiding question.

Is anything real?

Ocean

Even in summer it was cold.
We approached it, my brother and I,
dove into its changeable waves.
Here we learned to swim

away from our father's blue-white arms.
The cold grew inside us,
compelling us farther.

The Dark Sky

The explosions we heard that day
are silent in outer space. The sky
has no memory of numbers,

nor of phone numbers,
dog tags, zip codes,
not the dimmest memory.

With no end to the stars,
it's impossible to compare
the universe to ourselves,

so let's avoid comparisons altogether,
the way a physician
avoids a final diagnosis.

Ancient Egyptians believed the heart
stored memory; they mummified it too
inside the body, then buried everything

along with cat, dice, and spinning tops—
pastimes and memory
bundled together in hemp.

This pallet you and I lie on
is made of longing—
how we love to yearn!

And what's love hurrying us to—
a house of clouds? I guess
we evaporate. We fear it.

It's the knife we dare not touch,
the knife that pierces fog—
though I can't say why.

At Shore's Edge

Father yelled for him to come back.
He'd been there since when?

Far out, a dot. Face down.
Flimsy red raft, wind picking up.

Since midday,
when he'd woken, tumbled
into the water. And now,

was he asleep?
It was nearly sunset.

Everyone stood waving and ran along
the beach like sandpipers.

He liked speed.

Brother

Because he can't tell his own story—

      may he never sleep another night in jail.
      May he never shiver heroin sweat, flea-bitten, rib-broken.

Because he forgot that we'd walked with our dog—

      may he never forget the blue-spotted salamanders
      we found in muddy banks,
      or how we swung by the rope into those rough waves.

      May he sing all night, dream of a sunflower woman.

And let me forgive him, brother and consolation—

      though he dealt me a bad hand,
      and the price rose.

Let me not forget him, brother and sorrow—

      returned from prison, those five years
      engulfing him like a rubber suit,

his cheerless eyes pondering me—

my every fortune.

Flowers

Once they arrived without a card.

The man I rented a room from took them,
hoping they were his.

I knew they were for me.
It was wintry gray, and I needed
the red and blue anemones.

Those years irony meant nothing to me,
I traveled from one country to another,

searching for a pear tree
supported by ladders.

Room With Map

Where he leaned against pillows to laugh or weep,
there was only the smell of antiseptic.
No more breath of fire, breath of forgiveness,
no gods to whom we gave sacrifice,
the liver donor, and A-negative blood;
gone his wanting and mine.
The room was empty.
He was not returning.

In his desk, I found a plastic bag
with his broken prison Timex,
but couldn't stop the sycamore tree
from filling the windows of his apartment—
how the bark curled,
stained like an ancient map.

Barn Swallow

Shit streaks off the glass
and the swallow
shrieks from a near tree.
To see the eggs or the chicks,
whichever's in the nest—
on closer view, two nests side by side—

how to keep close and away?

The Other Branch

Across the Thanksgiving table, he announces his plan
to marry once more, then closes his eyes

and slides lower in his chair.
Is he sick? Nodding off?

So many of us—siblings, friends, his fiancée—appear in the
    chandelier's globe.
Pass the gravy, the cranberry or something, whatever it is.

       *

"Whatever it is has nothing to do with drugs," he says, opening
his eyes after the transplant. He's harbored in a mint-green gown,

and a nurse brings his methadone in a small cup.
"Tell me more about us," he says, "I'm falling asleep."

       *

I fall asleep in the hospital's Japanese garden
where orchids thrive on fogged glass shelves.

Awake, I lean close to see them:
each miniature face on its lithe stem.

*

Two live branches fall into a stream,
spiral—

the distance between us grows wider and wilder—

one branch spins far, faster than the other.

If I Remember Correctly

Memory is a wire that cuts—

    "I'll kill you," one brother hisses.
    A glass of milk hits the wall.

    "I can't save you," the other one whispers.
    "I can't save *me*."

    More boy than man, his light brown hair
    licks his neck, his good wool jacket.

    "I'll get you . . . I'll get you."
    What if he has a knife?—

or am I mistaken?

Mountain

My runaway brother returns.
He's been to the mountain
(meaning he's seen God);

finds me in my dorm, sophomore year,
and together, old friends, we talk
as a shadow enters the room.

Now I think it was a deity
acting the part of dusk,
though I hardly notice her—I'm happy

there beside him.
 "See how many needles I shot,"
and rolls his sleeve (meaning

he's kicked a drug habit,
meaning he had a habit)
and spills a cup of pencils—

clatter—my eyes shut. I don't
want to faint, fall.
The hash in his clay pipe

smells like glue,

not mountain pine.

Oh, his mind unfurls, he sings,

hums a little tune that will undo him.

Dusk splits the room in two.

Can I keep him, save him?

Blue embers fly, open a hole.

Deliverance Dream

The small, mute crowd of us,
now gathered, appears to float
across the tarmac to the terminal.

Under the flat, salt-colored sky, a heavy casket waits.

Lucky

The rabbi gestures to the congregation,
asks if there is anyone else who wants to speak.
My brother's best friend from his years in prison
jumps from a front-row seat.
Like a Yeshiva boy, his round pink cheeks flush
as he hesitates, uncertain.
In two long strides, all of us hushed,
he stands by the blue curtain,
raises his arms to say—he will never understand
why he is the lucky one.

That I understand.

Every year he calls on my brother's birthday,
until he doesn't or can't.

After Goethe's "Erl-King"

He was a boy
who couldn't keep from falling,
a ping in a bucket,
then the bucket overflowed.

In prison he washed in a bucket,
paid for his misconduct.
He was a bucket with a hole
that couldn't be patched.

Grain, water, wisdom
slid through that crack.
He never said he was scared,
caught red-handed with his desire.

Somehow, I'll forget how he slips
from his father's arms into fire.

Stone Lion

The lion at the family mausoleum lies still,
mossy-backed and obedient.
When no one watched, I rode it.

I never thought of those buried,
only wanted to escape the living
who were so easily offended.

Our grandfather hated the place:
"When everyone you know is dead,
you won't like it either."

The lion stares from the cemetery bed.
No one mounts the statue. It's silence
that's offensive, banging up against the sky.

II.

A Blessing

Already the air had begun to fry,
yet it was just cool enough for us

to jog the few blocks to Vihara Maha Devi Park
where your father's heart failed.

I met the gaze of the street sweeper, staring
at your bare legs, my naked arms—his spit landed close.

A new twelve-foot corrugated fence
hid the squatters from our sight

though nothing can hide my pale skin or the smell
of plastic burning from copper wire,

which isn't the only smell of desperation.
Do you remember standing by the bench,

trees filled with sleeping bats?
Buddha watched behind his plaster lids:

those who wash and drink in these fountains,
and those who stand motionless, wrapped in white.

He knows the spot where your father fell.
All equal in the Buddha's blessings!

May He Find Nirvana
May we find Nirvana.

But I get ahead of myself....

Auguries

*

Oh my brother,
no more your orphan mouth.
Why can't I kneel and pray?

I let myself out the window, take the fire escape.
The days pant.
The days hang.

*

He vanishes like water
through my fingers,

but he wasn't made of water or light
though he seemed lucent, tender—

after the evening bath, the child
who wrapped a towel turban-style

on his head, joked,
"I'm delightful to be with."

He was right
about the war

and I was a pedantic twerp.
He ate mayonnaise sandwiches,

played trumpet, then flute,
disappeared into the dog's luxuriant fur,

whip and speed of ocean surf,
devoured our mother's ice-cream wafer cake,

licking the whisk she'd hand him.
The poet Horace told his friend not to weep,

"It's all superfluous, I won't be there."
This is a reliquary

to hold my brother's gifts—
his sad kindness.

What to say to those who remember him?
I wait to hear him praised.

*

What led him to that outermost gate:
our absent father,
our violent, eldest brother?

One blames the mother, at least
that's what ours thought—

". . . don't wear that.
No one will ever love you . . .
you look like trash."

Mother—
who brought the grown child home,
stayed awake with him strung out,
shallow-breath'd,

who stored his methadone
on her refrigerator shelf.

*

Our elder brother weeps,
back shaking,

he looks like a crow,
hiking his shoulders,
raised for flight—

his red hair dyed blue-black.

*

She looks out the window hung with sky.
Tears mark her brown suede jacket,

slide from the creased face and wide mouth,
from her neck

to her hands;
from her dovelike body,

her dark head, fine hair,
the sharp smell of her

as she bends over me, my hand
patting her back; she stares

at a point beyond this,
twists papers my father demands she sign

and gives in, forsakes
her older boys—they will live with their father.

At a flash in the sky, she beckons her sons
back into the room

as if they might come
like music through a window.

*

I find a cache of love letters. Airmail paper still crisp:

I've found a home for us, sunny and cheap

On which occasions does she reread these letters?
Each time they go to court?

Kitten, I'm confident you're not pregnant

Each time my two older brothers run away, steal, deal drugs,
are sent to rehab, psych ward, prison?

I've bought a navy pinstriped suit for the wedding

Below my father's signature, she has appended with age-old scorn:

Had a wife, he couldn't keep her . . .

*

The house is divided.

Descended from gray wolves, our affectionate dog barks, guards the *domus*.

Wide-mouthed mother packs the linen drapes, takes my younger brother
and me.

Far-sighted father takes the ivory chest and older boys.

The dog of the era is left behind to shepherd, dig the rat hole by the
brook, to pace, retreat, and wail.

Dying, my mother asks,

"What madness was I thinking—to forget that dog?"

*

"You won't want it when you have it," she says.

The light bulb gives no heat,
the lukewarm batter never sets,
nothing bakes in the toy oven.

She knows the folly of desire.
I am too old for make-believe,
but she buys it because
I've lost father, brothers, house, and dog.

*

Driving half-lit, snowy streets
the cabbie says, "Keep fingers off glass."

From the rearview mirror swing bronzed baby shoes.
Whose are those? Who are we,

shuttled from home to home, knapsacks rattling on the seat,
two mice in a tin.

My baby brother's fingers leap on glass,
ghosts jump from the past.

Reading Montaigne, *How to Live*

Under the green umbrella, Death
sits, hoofing up
grass, drinking sangria.
"I'll call again tomorrow.
Make sure you're ready."

"Okay," I answer, watering
grass seed under the maples.

III.

Via Negativa

This time I won't think, *The sky is falling*
while riding the bus to Rikers Island.

In the prison waiting room, no guard will touch
my shoulder, say, "Why so scared?"

This time I won't be afraid,
won't flinch, won't shudder,

cameras won't seek us,
clicking from every corner,

and he won't ask if I have it,
and I won't have it

pressed into my sneaker, dope
(like me) closed in a yellow balloon.

Reading Basho (What I Call His "Drinking" Songs)

Cocaine vial
catches my eye. A voice calls—
crystal vein.

Makes you feel
like a god and alive. You
can't be both.

Sing Sing

"Why? Why?"

She wants me to stay overnight in a prison trailer.
The three of us—mother, son, daughter.
They let you do that, the family together.
I refuse.

We stand in the visitors line, our two brown bags
filled with fruit, salami, cartons of cigarettes.
Snow drifts into our shoes.

Prison construction exceeds all other industry.
One of the years he's inside is declared
New York State's Year of the Prison.

Sister

He's one more man
lit with prison fluorescence.

The day he's released, he welcomes me,
"What took you so long?"

Tears in my mouth.
Feckless, I think.

Dressed in street clothes, he looks well enough.
My arm around him, the prodigal,

I bring him to our father's house.
Oh, I'm not so different from the bitter sibling.

Boy

He played with fire,
lit matches by the dozens,
hid the tinder beneath his bed.
Three years older than I, he took my hand
at the crossroad, stood between me
and our elder brother,
sounded words I couldn't read,
and buried himself in sand
for me to trip over.

Harvest

"He's got cirrhosis—
another bag of vomit
I'll have to swallow."

The yellow moon looked as if it wanted
to pop, its innards colliding
with our landscape.

Afterimage

My mother dies and I ignore the bulbs
as they sprout in cold storage.
Anemic white stalks.

Later, given dirt and light,
an amaryllis chorus.
Crimson ladies,

red trumpet throats dissolving to black.

First Snow

If she were alive, I'd telephone.
She at her window,
I at mine
as snow falls aslant.

She at her window,
headlights sweeping out the old year
as snow falls aslant.
Into my hands rushes her voice

again, as headlights sweep out the old year.
I hear her, "Come right now!"
Into my hands rushes her voice
the night he died. There was an ice storm.

I hear her, "Come now!"
Nothing could be done. I waited
the night my brother died. Ice storm.
Couldn't survive.

Could we be done? Wait.
At dawn I drove to the city
he couldn't survive
and found her shaken, aghast.

Dawn, I drove to the city,
she was alone at last,
shaken, aghast,
she was at last mine.

She was alone,
a diffused mine,
at last she was mine,
an excavated mine.

If she were alive today, I'd call.

Hiking

I try to understand
why countless, unnamed pollutants

poison our air; how millions of dollars
were spent marketing opiates.

Get in the swing, with OxyContin. . . .
The mountain path ends in rock.

Hiking, I break my walking stick.
It's replaceable. There's a silence

that's like unspoken complaints,
two minds not making amends.

At the meadow's edge, a scarlet tanager
alights on a white pine—

are there words for us, America,
high on an uppermost branch?

Dear X Chromosome

I have the sense we are alone.

Found in ordinary cells, the extra
X makes the woman,
makes heart, breast, womb.

Why there's all this space inside me, I don't know.

Kidney, pancreas, stomach, spleen,
our hundred thousand miles of veins—
another universe unknown.

It takes three days to reach our moon.

Despite knowing we may be alone,
my arms and legs outstretch,
I keep trying to solve for X.

Ancient mothers live inside this X.

With all this space inside me,
X chromosome, mother ship, mitochondria
live inside this X.

Everything beautiful is far away and unknown.

I own the ancient mother X,
the message from my deep space
repeats inside the rocket ship.

Is There a Certainty of It?

If so I'll be the mother of the waiting room
where every *no* will rejoin its *yes,*
every breast hold the child it once fed.
I'll be the tyrant of bandages, keeper of salves,
every knife shall remember the wound,
and the tattoo relinquish its prisoner's skin.

I'll be paste and tape.
I'll be the oak's merciful shade.
I'll be the gate to its comings
and goings, the quick hush of it.

IV.

After Daniel Chester French's *Angel of Death Staying the Hand of the Young Sculptor*

There comes a time when I can't look.
The Angel, with her sweeping, feathered wings,

is too real. I no longer believe in angels
or that she snatched life from the young sculptor.

Abraded by time and weather, her vague face stays hooded,
while his countenance remains sharp and lively.

How spirited his body appears beneath the stone apron
that protects him from dust.

There comes a time when I stop asking why.
Reasons flake away.

I'm not even looking at them,
someone else has my eye—

I just don't want to see their fingers touch,
the chisel taken from his hand.

Yahrzeit

At this cliff edge, bench engraved
with your name, Brother,
Father and I stand. Sorrow
and relief spring like wild onions
from his startled eyes.
"I have to live with this," he says,
his downturned mouth brings
your half-lived life to mind.
Goodbye, now.
We've come with offerings, words
in honor of you
whom I shall see no more.
Accept these sister-tears shed for you.

Leveraged Hearts

Swimming beside my friend
in the town pool, she tells me

her dead mother and my dead
brother are together, talking.

Her mother: "You look like a corpse in a tuxedo."
My brother: "With that attitude, you'll never leave Limbo."

I hurry from the pool, wrap myself in a big dry towel.

Transit

Where are we headed?
Here's the corridor.

Where are we headed?
Listen for footfall.

Where are we headed?
Rain on the deck.

Where are we headed?
Cross yourself.

Sri Lanka

Newly wedded, we borrowed two Schwinns
from the Rest House and rode into the jungle.

He hurried ahead on the road
like a moon wandering a cold sky.

I was in his country for the first time.
He sped on, his white shirt aglow.

I tried to ignore the young soldiers lifting their rifles,
the monkeys in trees throwing stones;

a water buffalo turned its head as we passed
the reservoir where women washed their hair;

stone pillars elbowed from weeds,
and the sun flamed out.

The Bo tree we circled—grown from a sapling
of Buddha's tree, another transplant—

was draped with flags, roots
half-buried by incense ash and lottery stubs.

Hundreds of years ago, a monk carved
these words on a rock to his beloved:

Talk to me gently of your heart   impenetrable

I seek you in the monk's arcane verse,
the improbable evidence of things I long to see

like those who hold oil lamps to light the road.

Temple of the Relic

Like an article of faith, the camera is slung
over his chest. We enter
through hoops of metal detectors, soldiers
search bags and frisk our children.
Shoes at the threshold, we walk barefoot
into a labyrinth, our offerings tumbling
onto piles of lotus a thousand petals deep.
Told that Buddha's tooth is hidden in a casket
at the center of the temple, we leave
the fresh air, the view of the lake,
tourists reborn as pilgrims.

In the inner chamber, pyres of candles and incense,
the room reeks of ash and sweat.
We huddle, our prayer inching along strings
of flags, messages looped and tied to every timber and ledge.
We chant the names of our loved ones
and the ones lost, the ones who are restless, unable to sleep.
Their names thrum in us.
We say their names that they may rest,
we say their names that we may sleep.

Fable

O my children, the ant has a boulder in its mouth.
Pale-white ant rushes with a potato chip
that fell yesterday from our table.

I was like that once—moving rapidly—
taking food home, bearing the weight

because an ant is a lever, its body a physics,
the weight of the chip is nothing to it.

O wonders of the world, I am nothing
compared to the work.

Postcolonial

A Dutch cabinet opens:
rush of mildew.
"It's the sea," he says.
Hair plump as a watered bush,
he paces the house he was born in
as if a part of him
unsuited for an emigrant's life
had remained stored with the batik shirts
in the sandalwood almirah.
Tying his orange-and-black sarong
around his waist, he surveys
the garden, returns to the veranda.
This man, the son of the son of the
son of, etc.—and a sari halves my stride.
Aunties and uncles wish us
happy homecoming; bring
tea packets, and ashtrays
hammered into a teardrop shape.
Love from Ceylon!
I tell them we don't smoke.
They shake their heads *no*, meaning *yes*.

Three a.m. jetlag: he's reading
his father's old letters in the near-dark office.

On the desk there's a typewriter,
no fingerprints on its keys,
and from a black and white photo,
one arm waving, his father
appears to be calling.
A son could do so much for his country.
Yes, I say, meaning *no*.

Days of Cinnamon Gardens

Saturdays, our neighbors cooked dal curry
and whoever had time sat on the veranda
drinking beer and turned the reddening chilies,
listening to a kettle sputter mutinous thoughts.
Late at night the kids ran between houses waving
incense sticks like Fourth of July sparklers.

Into the neighborhood someone passed a recipe
calling for a spice such as gunpowder. Someone called
for a dash more charcoal, more cayenne, more smoke.
A man climbed the jack tree one night
and a football-sized bomb exploded in the garden.
On Biera Lake, hundreds of coconuts floated downstream

like heads. Our neighbors hid in someone's pantry closet;
the North road blocked. *The peace is blown to smithereens!*
politicians shouted. Fear has a smell,
like the mold on books and walls. Guns,
on the market once more, and ammo—
costlier than ever—were carried in hemp sacks.

Our friends sent out their children to safer countries,
and we didn't return the next year or the next. . . .
At the end of the millennium, the morning *Times*

showed us our gentle neighbor's face—
his car had yielded at the park where an unknown woman
bowed to him and detonated the bomb she wore.

The red hibiscus hedge regrew—frenetic bloom of sadness.

At Night

Roads lead into
and away from the fort.

Hours pass. Years might
pass. Rain, rain, sun—

if change is everywhere, I am
in despair; I see nothing of it—

Translation

In English we come to grief—
and drive drunk over a cliff—

or it befalls us—a stroke
or lightning—and we grieve.

A famous translator said to her students,
"Tend the fire!"

—every word born with its sphere of heat.
"Look up from your pages!"

was another phrase she'd say. Both at once—
like riding a bicycle with no hands.

At her desk, the translator rapped a dictionary
absently, searching for a pattern

as she mourned her son's accidental death—
an absurd event.

The heat searches for us.
Last night, every leaf blew off the linden tree.

This morning it's filled with ravens
flapping their jewel-black wings, lifting off—

Brother Again

I knew the time was coming
when he'd be free, one of the many
rising over the tree line, over yards,
waving down at Mrs. McCarthy,
the crossing guard below,
halting cars on Old Army Road
and gliding in the soundlessness above
street and traffic, steering
toward his castle, even now.

Mother

I feel her bubble up
from sidewalk pavement.

She who causes tremors,
causes unfolding.

Forsythia, black hellebore,
rude crocus.

Then a breeze flits, a daub,
a caress, a wink.

Headstone

The living need such tending!

What about the dead?

Carefree,
no interest
in an eye for an eye.

Bull's-eye!

Notes

"The Dark Sky" is for Anita Glesta, whose multimedia installation *Gernika/Guernica* explores connections between the bombing of the village of Guernica, 1937, and the attack of the World Trade Center, 2001.

"A Blessing." Vihara Maha Devi Park is located at Independence Square, Colombo, Sri Lanka.

"Reading Montaigne, *How to Live*." Sarah Bakewell's biography, *How to Live: A Life of Montaigne in One Question and Twenty Attempts at an Answer,* offers an inspired introduction to Montaigne.

"Hiking." "Get into the Swing, With OxyContin" was the jingle used by Purdue Pharma to promote OxyContin.

"Dear X Chromosome" was written to accompany Xin Liu's video installation, *Living/Distance* performed at the MAX 2019 Space Festival in San Francisco. "Why there's all this space inside me / I don't know" is taken from Wislawa Szymborska's poem, "A Large Number."

"Yahrzeit" is based on Catullus 101.

"Days of Cinnamon Gardens" is in memory of Neelan and Sithie Tiruchelvam.

"Translation." The lines quoted are Svetlana Geier's (1923-2010), who translated the works of Dostoyevsky into German, and taken from Vadim Jendreyko's brilliant documentary, *The Woman With the Five Elephants*, which portrays Geier and her practice.

Acknowledgments

I wish to thank my teachers for their inspiration and constant faith,
most especially Ellen Bryant Voigt, Martha Rhodes, Joan Aleshire, and
Eleanor Wilner.

I thank my fellow artists and friends who have generously given their time
and insights: Catherine Barnett, Maudelle Driskell, Elizabeth England,
Alva Greenberg, Anita Glesta, Elizabeth T. Gray, Jr., Kimiko Hahn,
Iris Hanika, Joel Hinman, Maeve Kinkead, Alex Knox, Krys Lee,
Arden Levine, Margaree Little, David Lynn, Deb McAlister,
Emily McKeage, Lita Moses, Kira Obolensky, J. J. Penna, Carl Phillips,
Alicia Jo Rabins, Anna Duke Reach, Amy Schiffman, and
Mary Jo Thompson.

My heartfelt thanks to Martha Rhodes, Ryan Murphy, Sally Ball, and
Clarissa Long at Four Way Books, to the alumni of the MFA Program for
Writers at Warren Wilson College, and to my friends at the *Kenyon Review*.

Thanks to my family for their love.

I am grateful to the editors of the journals, anthologies, and books in
which earlier versions of some of these poems were published, including
*Bodega Magazine, The Cortland Review, Disquieting Muses Quarterly Review,
Epiphany Literary Journal, Faultline: Journal of Art & Letters, Kenyon Review
Online, The Madison Review, Mead Magazine,* and *New Orleans Review.*
"Fable," was republished in *Buzz Words, Poetry of Insects,* The Everyman's
Anthology of Poems. Earlier drafts of "Thanksgiving," "Mountain,"
and "*Via Negativa*" were published in *Lost Orchard: prose & poetry from the
Kirkland College Community;* "If There Is A Certainty of It," appeared in
The Traveler's Mecum: A Poetry Anthology; earlier versions of "Postcolonial,"
appeared in *AP English Literature & Composition for Dummies,* and was
republished in *The Writers Studio at 30.*

Abigail Wender's poems and translations have been published in numerous journals. She holds a degree from the MFA Program for Writers at Warren Wilson College. *Reliquary* is her first collection of poems. She lives in New York City.

Publication of this book was made possible by grants and donations. We are also grateful to those individuals who participated in our 2020 Build a Book Program. They are:

Anonymous (14), Robert Abrams, Nancy Allen, Maggie Anderson, Sally Ball, Matt Bell, Laurel Blossom, Adam Bohannon, Lee Briccetti, Therese Broderick, Jane Martha Brox, Christopher Bursk, Liam Callanan, Anthony Cappo, Carla & Steven Carlson, Paul & Brandy Carlson, Renee Carlson, Cyrus Cassells, Robin Rosen Chang, Jaye Chen, Edward W. Clark, Andrea Cohen, Ellen Cosgrove, Peter Coyote, Janet S. Crossen, Kim & David Daniels, Brian Komei Dempster, Matthew DeNichilo, Carl Dennis, Patrick Donnelly, Charles Douthat, Morgan Driscoll, Lynn Emanuel, Monica Ferrell, Elliot Figman, Laura Fjeld, Michael Foran, Jennifer Franklin, Sarah Freligh, Helen Fremont & Donna Thagard, Reginald Gibbons, Jean & Jay Glassman, Ginny Gordon, Lauri Grossman, Naomi Guttman & Jonathan Mead, Mark Halliday, Beth Harrison, Jeffrey Harrison, Page Hill Starzinger, Deming Holleran, Joan Houlihan, Thomas & Autumn Howard, Elizabeth Jackson, Christopher Johanson, Voki Kalfayan, Maeve Kinkead, David Lee, Jen Levitt, Howard Levy, Owen Lewis, Jennifer Litt, Sara London & Dean Albarelli, David Long, James Longenbach, Excelsior Love, Ralph & Mary Ann Lowen, Jacquelyn Malone, Donna Masini, Catherine McArthur, Nathan McClain, Richard McCormick, Victoria McCoy, Ellen McCulloch-Lovell, Judith McGrath, Debbie & Steve Modzelewski, Rajiv Mohabir, James T. F. Moore, Beth Morris, John Murillo & Nicole Sealey, Michael & Nancy Murphy, Maria Nazos, Kimberly Nunes, Bill O'Brien, Susan Okie & Walter Weiss, Rebecca Okrent, Sam Perkins, Megan Pinto, Kyle Potvin, Glen Pourciau, Kevin Prufer, Barbara Ras, Victoria Redel, Martha Rhodes, Paula Rhodes, Paula Ristuccia, George & Nancy Rosenfeld, M. L. Samios, Peter & Jill Schireson, Rob Schlegel, Roni & Richard Schotter, Jane Scovell, Andrew Seligsohn & Martina Anderson, James & Nancy Shalek, Soraya Shalforoosh, Peggy Shinner, Dara-Lyn Shrager, Joan Silber, Emily Sinclair, James Snyder & Krista Fragos, Alice St. Claire-Long,

Megan Staffel, Bonnie Stetson, Yerra Sugarman, Dorothy Tapper Goldman, Marjorie & Lew Tesser, Earl Teteak, Parker & Phyllis Towle, Pauline Uchmanowicz, Rosalynde Vas Dias, Connie Voisine, Valerie Wallace, Doris Warriner, Ellen Doré Watson, Martha Webster & Robert Fuentes, Calvin Wei, Bill Wenthe, Allison Benis White, Michelle Whittaker, and Ira Zapin.